AT THE BUREAU OF DIVINE MUSIC

a light as of the end of the boulevards

Wallace Stevens

AT THE BUREAU

OF DIVINE MUSIC

POEMS BY

MICHAEL

HEFFERNAN

WAYNE STATE UNIVERSITY PRESS

DETROIT

15 14 13 12 11   5 4 3 2 1

Library of Congress Cataloging-in-Publication Data

Heffernan, Michael, 1942–

At the bureau of divine music : poems / by Michael Heffernan.

p. cm. — (Made in Michigan writers series)

ISBN 978-0-8143-3510-9 (alk. paper)

I. Title.

PS3558.E413A95 2011

811'.54—dc22

2010028318

∞

Designed and typeset by Maya Rhodes
Composed in Horley Old Style MT

For Ann

Contents

The Dove

All morning and from half the night before,
either the dove was there or in a dream
making its hapless moan despite the pain
some listener might lend to listen in
or, comforting himself with what the boughs
might bless him with, if he could raise to them
a hand of blessing, offer his pain in kind
to seem the dove's own likeness, wings becalmed,
small heart unbroken yet, and a bird's soul
incapable of mourning or desire.

Save Yourself

After I wander the morning in circles
trying to find my way back to the old house
where I left you lingering in the back halls
feasting your eyes on more of the numinous,
it's the bête noire, the sacred cow I'm chasing
into a blind alley where cornering her
turns her around—and then I do the gnashing—
I stand my ground—I have had it up to here—
but instead of ripping her face off, I go
straight out the door I open where her mouth is
onto gorgeous springtime in a sparkling meadow
abuzz with dragonflies, asplotch with shadows
shaken from hawks risen out of their bodies.
I never felt such happiness before this.

Campanile

This radical inquiry into things
beneath or far outside the look of them
invites a lapidary stratagem
to stop the eyes and heart from wanderings
beyond where they can reach. Extended wings
or not, one bird is maddened to have come
close to the downswing something keeps him from,
then lifts him noiseless back where his mate sings
voluptuary offerings a gust
of wind beats into blather. What is left
raggedly replicates what it all meant
before the lights came on and the sky went:
two pigeons backed up crazy and bereft
to huddle in the cold as creatures must.

The Scent of Rose Water

A snake sneaked into the jungle behind the brownstone
on the Lower East Side where we all still lived.
It was an anaconda crossed with a silverfish
whose tendrils shimmered from the cherry tree
in the little dooryard behind the summer kitchen.
When his clumsy partner-in-crime the armadillo came
to help him attack the children and my wife and me,
I absented myself in search of the rifle that I kept
in the great house on Jefferson Street in the Seventies.
I climbed up through the door to the stairway
that wound into the secret loft on the third floor,
where I used to watch for you through the curved panes.
The gun was bigger and rustier than I remembered
from the last time I took it from the closet under the eaves.
A lovely little nickel-plated pistol also found itself
in my loose-fitting Army jacket, where it went off
and blew apart its pocket and a hole in my jeans,
barely missing the flesh of my right thigh,
which would have crippled me, but instead I ran
all the way from Kansas to New York City
with the whole right leg of my jeans on fire.
The snake and the armadillo had removed elsewhere.
You stood in the pewter light of the dining area
arranging a spray of lyrical hibiscus on the water
that you had poured into a crystal bowl
from your mother's silver pitcher engraved with the line
A Thing of Beauty Is a Joy Forever.
The bowl had been her Aunt Elizabeth's.
Except for the little girl who died at home
and was buried in a shoebox in the garden,

all Aunt Elizabeth's children had been given up.
I only wanted to lay eyes on you.
We might have begun to shine in the meantime.

Tahiti

When you and your Jack Russell were moving in,
I knew the time had come to begin my life
as the neighborhood Gauguin. So I covered
ten prestretched 20×16 canvases
with blobs of phthalo and alizarin.
I wanted a whole roll next, to stretch myself
on leftover tomato stakes. Better yet,
I would go down to the wharf where the cargo ships
docked every month with goods in gunnysacks
to be unsewn, resewn, and stretched
for an authentic surface on which to beguile
the afterlife with women clad in nothing.
I had the little dog sketched in my head
for the lower right-hand corner where Seurat
put the monkey on the string, except Jacqueline
would be sniffing the foot of a man just leaving.
Burlap was easier to find eventually,
for $1.99/yd at the fabric store,
to be tacked to an old pallet and painted on,
stiffened with ordinary paint-shop primer.
I considered whether anyone would get
the Gauguinesque homage—which had to do
with why Gauguin wanted to leave his flat
with its walls affecting a slick palm-forest green,
around the corner from St-Germain-des-Prés,
to sail to Tahiti the second time,
on the way to the Marquesas. Gauguin had
something different to do in the South Seas
when he went back than what he went there for
after the wife ran home to Copenhagen.

He needed a place to die, and tried to,
with arsenic that he neglected to ask the chemist
how to make it give him more than a queasy stomach
and a sleepless night on the mountain by himself.

The Way You Do

You caught me at a bad time, when things were weird,
and bound to get weirder with you around.
What you call love can make me really crazy.
My ex did that, only a different way.
He would come home to have sex at lunchtime,
no matter what was going on with me.
The kids could be frying cats in the track-light sockets,
after turning the broken bulbs into kitty food,
in case they couldn't kill them some other way;
or crucifying a neighbor kid in the backyard,
or using the custom-built treehouse as a gallows
for each other; or I could be doing laundry,
and he'd walk in and lead me to the bedroom.
Then he'd have lunch and go back to his patients.
We'd do it at night too, and in the morning.
He even wanted it once when I was sick.
I had the flu. He said it was his right.
He screwed around on me, eventually,
and told me so. He seemed to think I'd like it.
He got his jollies watching me come apart
with stuff he even brought to bed with us.
He thought it got me off. Maybe it did.
There's quite a lot here I'm not telling you.
Maybe you get it, which is what your look
is trying to tell me now, but I don't think so.
You're very good at making me think so.
Lately I've noticed how your look has changed.
You're too intense for me. I could be crazy,
but this is something you refuse to see.
Of course I'm pissed at you, and I don't know why.

You're not as funny as you used to be.
Sometimes I think you're crazier than I am.

You know I told you about how I went
to Mark Wood at his Chevy dealership
and said I wanted him to sleep with me.
We had been good friends for twelve years by then.
People would notice us at gatherings.
My husband caught us at a party once
at our house. Mark had gone to find his coat
in the bedroom. I came up from behind
to run my hand inside his shorts. My husband
walked in to use the bathroom. There I was
with my fist around Mark's cock, and his one arm
in one sleeve and the other sleeve hanging loose
next to my elbow like he's grabbing my ass,
and my husband says, "You two look really friendly.
Why don't you use the bed after I'm done?"
I went back to the party, and Mark left.
Later, after I caught my husband screwing
the French teacher from the high school, and I filed,
I waited a couple months with him still around
and sleeping on the sofa. He wouldn't leave.
I went to Mark Wood's Chevy dealership.
I walked right into his office in the back.
I told him I was feeling vulnerable.
I needed to feel like a woman once again.
I said I wanted us to go to bed.
It shouldn't matter any more than that,
since we were friends. He took me up on it.

We went on over to his place and fucked,
an hour before I had to pick my kids up.
We did that every afternoon for a month,
mostly at his house, once or twice at mine,
after the kids were gone. I'd be doing laundry
to wash the sheets from Mark when my husband came,
in case he tried to do me like before.
One night he got in bed with me, just to sleep.
He couldn't get good sleep on the sofa.
I let him stretch beside me. Around that time,
Mark went to the Islands. After he came back,
he changed his phone and got a private number.
He told some people that he hated me.

A friend from Garden Club was shot in bed
by someone who hated her enough to kill her.
A neighbor found her sidewise on her pillow
with tissue and bone where her head used to be.
Half of her face was left, like a mask of skin.
She seemed to be laughing in a funny dream.
Whoever it was had taken a revolver
and shot her through the French doors from the terrace
of her big house by the Lake when she was alone.
That could have been me. Sometimes I wake up
in the middle of the night and I hear laughter,
but it isn't mine. It could be Mark Wood laughing
after he puts a bullet in my mouth
from the gun I'm eating in the dream he laughs in.

I hated Mark Wood once, when he took up
with someone else we knew and wouldn't tell me.

He said I was still sleeping with my husband,
after I got the settlement I wanted
and the new house he paid for. The truth is
I loved my husband, but I could not stand
to have him put his hands on me after a while.
He kept on wanting me. He begged for me.
He said it was just sport-fucking with the others,
but with me it was like worship at the temple.
There wasn't any way I'd fall for that.
Eventually all I wanted was Mark Wood
and a nice life, along with all the stuff
my husband had agreed to give to me.
I wanted what I knew belonged to me
that women like me get from men like them.
I wanted the peace of mind that comes about
when a woman finds her own place in her skin.
I couldn't tell how many parts of me
caught fire to feel the pang of who I am.
My husband wasn't going to find out,
or else I'd lose my kids, which would have killed me.

I really loved Mark Wood. I love you too.
I love you, but I'm not in love with you.
And that's a problem I can't fix right now.
There's a pathology here we can't get past.
This isn't about you, or about me.
It isn't about you or me or us.
What it's about is crazy, weird, and sad.
Mark made me laugh. You used to make me laugh.
We both stopped laughing a long time ago.
You used to make me laugh when we made love.

One night, you threw my arms over the bed
with one leg on your shoulder, one of your legs
around my other leg, the way you do.
I started coming with you, and you screamed.
Then I began to scream; we both were screaming.
It was so funny that I started laughing.
Next thing I knew I kicked the floor lamp over,
and down it crashed. There was glass everywhere.
I said, "Oh shit," and I apologized,
right then, and kept on coming, hard, and then
we both were laughing like we couldn't stop.
You said it was fun to fuck and break things.
I said so too. Now all we do is break things.
Everyone's broken. I know I've broken you.
You'd break me if you could, but I won't let you.

The Empress

It had become clear that the only way
to rid her from our faces was to kill her.
Apart from what she always did for us,
we still could be an easygoing lot
of negligible ingrates. The fact that she
had offered us our freedom from desire
in a world made plentiful by her largesse,
granting us all the gift of who she was—
combined with her insufferable presumption
to owning those she gave the things she owned—
fastened us to one common frame of mind
that bodied forth the doing of the deed.
Everyone's eyes were wide with rectitude
when this imperative belonged to me.
I took the matter up with energy
befitting my disdain. Her dropping over
later that weekend fell in perfectly
with inclinations to perform some act
that graced a naked aptitude for rage.
She came to sit and smoke as usual,
filling the kitchen nook with talk of how
she knew my heart better than anyone,
because, of course, she had the means to know it,
which was true enough for her, and me as well,
if she said so, and kept on saying so
in words that spun like the blue clouds that rose
above her chair out of her great toad's head,
which, in mid-word, I wrenched by its black hair
to snap her neck as clean as a dry stick
against the top rung, having stepped up behind

just as her cackle from a thought she loved
had spasmed enough to let her think again
and start to say whatever I might have learned,
had I the hunger to keep listening.
She always put her feet up on the table,
so when her face looked at me upside down,
her feet flew up and kicked the kitchen lamp,
which leapt and wobbled wildly as she dropped
onto the floor. I smoothly stepped aside.
Then everyone filed in from the next room.
They took turns guessing what she might have said
if she had caught the breath to let me know.
One of them thought it no doubt had to do
with how much she enjoyed being filthy rich,
as often her grotesque self-satisfaction
led her to blurt with candid gaiety.
Now she is filthy dead, somebody added,
expecting laughter, but nobody laughed.
Insouciance like a god's had come instead
to fill the place with new tranquility
and bring the gift of easeful liberty
that we had no one but ourselves to thank for.
Something was here that had to do with love
that nobody understood, not even me.
After a while, I sat there by myself.
They carried her to her car and drove her home.
One of them called and said her dog had come
and curled up at her feet on the lounge chair
where they had stretched her by the swimming pool.
Her housekeeper would see her the next day

and go about her chores, not noticing
anything wrong, not even an odd smell.
Later I might stop over to drop off
the black sapphire I found on the kitchen floor.

The Message

My husband had a knack for knowing things.
I don't know how he knew about Jack and me,
unless he had me tailed. I think he did,
though he would never say. All I know is
one day the Company security
came by and told me to clean out my desk
and head for the parking lot. Something about
the use of company funds for personal business,
something about me and Jack that they found out
and wouldn't tell me how, and wouldn't tell me
which of us was the one that used the other.
Jack had been reprimanded. I was fired.
It had to be my husband. I never thought
the crazy bastard knew me well enough,
he was so stupidly in love with me.
He'd call me up when I was out of town
and tell me how he wished that he was there,
and there I'd be with Jack or someone else
reaching his hands around me from behind
trying to get inside me with his fingers.
One time I almost had to cry out loud.
My husband kept on talking and never noticed.
Finally I told him he didn't get the message.
This was in Dallas at the Anatole.
Jack had a towel on, I was in my robe.
My husband nearly cried he was so sick,
so painfully adoring, I almost told him
but didn't want to yet. There was no reason
to let him know what he should figure out.
I had a plan to meet Jack in Shreveport.
I called him at the chicken plant in Seguin—

on the 800 line, so it wouldn't show.
He ran the loading dock. He got his boss
to let him drive to pick me up in Shreveport
and take me to the plant, supposedly
on business. We both loved that part of it.
He turned in his mileage to the Company.
"We're really pulling a fast one," I told him.
"Why don't I sit and cross my legs and smile
and say to Randy, 'Thanks for letting Jack
come get me'?" Jack said no to that. Jack said
Randy was not the type to be amused.
"He'd kill me and care," Jack said. His sense of fun
stopped short where business and his job came in.
I understood, but that was not the point.
I told him I'd have new pink panties on,
maybe a new nightgown he could take off.
He said I wouldn't need one—I would spend
the whole time naked once I hit the door.
I said I'd work out doing deep knee bends
and eat nothing but vegetables till then.
He promised he would drink nothing but tea,
to get rid of the beer gut. Exercise
was out for now. He had an injury
from playing softball, and it hadn't healed.
He talked about his problems with Randy Wade
and how he needed to get out of there.
"I'll put my whole life in your hands," he said,
trying to make me sick with loving me.
I knew he wanted something, like they all did,
just like my husband always did. The fool
was so in love with me he never noticed

how much I had despised him all along.
All men are fools in love, without exception.
It turns them into boys, or idiots.
They never notice where the line is drawn
between the thing they want and what I'll give them.
Sometimes I'd take the trophy off the shelf,
the one I won when I was three years old
for being the prettiest little girl in town,
and I would rub it till a piece of it
got smooth enough to show my face, almost
the way it looked in 1962,
and I could tell something of what they saw,
a tiny part of what I must have been
and could have gone on being, had I known
when I was young and stupid what would happen
and what I stood to lose when I got older.
The things a man demands, the things a woman
gives to a man that can't be taken back.
I tried to tell them, but they wouldn't hear me.
My husband wasn't any different.
He'd come to bed when I was half asleep
and bring one hand up under my nightgown
to spread his fingers nipple to nipple.
Before I could hold back, the other hand
was opening my thighs and slipping in,
and off would come the nightgown, then his mouth
stopped me from even thinking to say no,
and he had made me his the umpteenth time,
convinced I loved him for the afterthought
that always came when he would say he loved me
so I would say the same when he was done.

He'd lie there with his elbow on my hip,
and kiss my shoulders, breathe into my hair,
or sniff my armpit, which he said smelled good.
Sometimes he'd rub his hand along my face
like a blind man trying to learn the way I looked.
I'd close my eyes and wait for him to stop.
Slowly his hand grew lighter and the dark
would swallow up his fingers and my face
quit throbbing. He would say goodnight,
then lift himself away and roll aside.
We'd drop off by ourselves, and sleep alone.
He must have seen our life continuing,
till one of us put the other in the ground,
and more than likely me that would bury him,
and what would I have left but my own grave
and no one home to put me into it.

Jack said he liked the pillows in Pine Bluff
better than Little Rock or Russellville.
In Pine Bluff we had two adjoining rooms
with four beds, so the pillows came to eight,
which put me high up like a harem girl,
while he went down below the way I liked it.
I grabbed him by his ears to bring him in,
to come inside me while I kept on coming,
till I lost count and we were soaking wet.
He loved to scrub his moustache in my tuft
like a soft brush that made me start to tingle
and jump a little while he rang my doorbell.
In Shreveport we went window-shopping first.
I knew he hated that. I hoped he would.

I wanted him to hate something at least,
so I could have him how I wanted him.
He wanted me for more reasons than one.
Two weeks before, he called me for a favor.
"You've got this inside track," he said. "Isn't it time
you did something for me?" My stomach turned
when he said that. I said I couldn't ask
too many favors. People would get suspicious,
and that would be the end of what they'd give me.
I could see him fingering his coffee cup
and tapping a pencil on the desk and thinking
"What can I get from her?" I stopped him dead.
I gave him my coldest major-player voice
and shut him up right there. "I'll put my whole
body in your hands," he said, after a pause.
"That's better," I said, in my sex-kitten voice.
He said he'd let me go, just for a while,
and couldn't wait to get me in Shreveport.
"Now, smile," he said, as if he had to know.
"I am," I said, and saw him sitting there
like a boy kicking his feet back and forth,
holding onto the porch swing with both hands
and staring up the street for the ice-cream man.
There isn't one of them that can get past
the need for something sweet to put their tongues in.

That night in Shreveport there was something else
I had to tell him. I had seen my doctor.
I wasn't about to let Jack know. Instead,
I told him he would have to use protection.

He threw a pack in with his cigarettes
at the Superette on our way back from dinner.
I'm not sure what he thought, but he thought twice
about going for his little extra treat.
I didn't want him asking if he could.
I gave my signal just to come inside,
and then I acted like he made me crazy.
I crawled back up the bed until my head
hung over and he knelt there with his knees
under my ribs and pushed me with it hard
and kept on pushing like he couldn't stop
or wouldn't, like he wanted me to beg
to get it over with and say good night.
I tried to squeeze on him. I stroked his balls.
I rubbed his ass. Nothing could make him stop.
He had become an instrument of torture
with a jackhammer at the end of it.
He wouldn't stop, no matter what I did.
Finally I thought I would pass out.
My head hurt and my neck was about to break.
I heard his voice. He said he liked the way
I looked without a head. And then he laughed.
He kept on laughing. I could feel him stretch
and then he burst, but there was nothing warm,
no sweet juice filling me over the brim,
just the cold air and Jack a long way off,
receding into nowhere, and me halfway
onto the floor, swallowed up in the dark.
I noticed the sharp smell of carpet cleaner.
And then a hand reached down to pull me up

and lay me down. Jack rolled back where he was
and went to sleep. I pulled the covers up
and let him sleep there naked, in the cold.

Next morning he was up before I was.
He waited for me in the parking lot.
He put me in the car without a word.
We hardly talked at all the whole way down.
He saw me to my room at the motel
and went home to his wife. He called me once
the next day on his way to pick me up
to drive me to the plane in San Antonio.
I didn't call him for a week or so.
By that time somebody had turned us in.
My husband had moved out, with all his stuff.
One day I talked to his voice mail. I said,
"You are a crazy mean son of a bitch.
You always have been one and always will be."
He called the house when I was gone. He said:
"I hope you find another line of work
or another crazy mean son of a bitch
like me to give you everything you want."
I played that message halfway through again,
then hit erase. I went to shut the blinds
over the sliding door to kill the light.
Out in the yard the cat was coming home
and crying for his dinner. The heat came on.
The blower made the blinds move side to side.

A Sudden Shower

A restorative walk in the garden, a rock in the shoe,
cantankerous clouds, a split-second view
of a bluebird lighting in the cherry tree, swallowing itself
among plump new leaves—all these were for you
and the incorruptible memory of your love.
I had awaked from night sweats and murderous dreams.
I held my head. I begged the cat to die.
I contemplated the smashed fly on the windowpane
above the sink. I got my coffee going. I said my prayers
to the small gods of plumbing, wiring, domestic engineering.
That cat would not die. She took to her duchy of dung
to build more cottages among its brooding hills.
The rain she made reminded her townspeople
of the merciless amenities. Dissimulations on that point
proved brutally useless. I had walked back in
from the garden without a clue
to the heartrending bluebird's whereabouts. As for you,
I surrendered your memory to the goodwives of Kittythorpe,
hugging their elbows at picket gates
by banks of bloodwort, henbane, dogtooth, wormwood,
scraps of you twisting into the rain.

Eclogue

The field across the road was beautiful.
I won't describe it. I went walking out
just now to see it. There was a huge white bird
that settled in the tree beside the fence.
Another swooped around on great brown wings.
I needed to preach to birds. And, naturally,
I had to sneeze, and naturally they flew.
The brown one simply vanished, while the white one
that had been in the tree slid off behind
and was halfway to the river when I saw him,
no bigger than a sparrow, disappearing.
So that was that. So I came back indoors
to watch the sky again out of my window
and think of you. I thought about a word
I found once in an Irish dictionary,
referring to the space between your fingers.
It also means the space between your toes.
I looked it up: *ladhar*—a metaphor
for the space between two rivers, roads, etc.
The problem, obviously, is how to say it.
The *–dh–* in the middle is the trick.
It's the voiced guttural spirant used in English
for the common death rattle and little else.
You have to try to gargle between the *a*'s
or cough the *l* around and past the *r*,
being careful not to spit up something foul
while trying to caress a certain place
with the tip of the tongue. I'm happy to do that
and say nothing about it—to keep my peace
and let the white bird light between two branches,

while the one with brown wings circles out of sight
above the field next to the river where I sit
helping you free your blouse from your elbows.

Africa

I looked out toward the pasture at the cows
making their way from unknown hinterlands
to find themselves a dark patch under trees
and look out toward the places they came from.
The shade was cool, the way shade often is
even in Africa, and Africa
was often what I thought, when I drove past
the pasture into town beyond the floodplain
where silent natives let their cattle move
among the egrets, geese, herons, and flies.
If this were Africa, what would I do
to live there? Would I simply roam about
from one place to another seeking shade
and company among the animals?
Should anyone attempt to live alone
in such a place as that? Would any place
be good enough to, without having to
pick up and wander continents from home?
Once when such thoughts went roaring through my head
before I got to the next house up the road,
where someone like me stood by a chain-link fence
and a row of pines an ancient neighbor planted
to keep folks out, I knew I had no reason
to watch those cows again. The man I saw
had something in his hand, a knife or gun.
I thought I watched him turning in the mirror
twirling a sword above his head and screaming.
Beyond the pines, the warrior disappeared
into the world he came from. A cross of light
shook among boughs of gloom. I had to move,
at least to put new things in front of me,

if not to make another kind of home,
if home was what I wanted in the first place.
I'd call it by its name if it had one,
or, failing that, I'd call it Africa.

Key

My Sunday morning nightmare takes me beyond
mystical towers and strident boulevards
to the underground whose priestesses lurch the halls,
shaking their fiery coifs around the latest
deranged advisories that they have to spew
onto the air to help me find my way
to the hotel with my luggage and your note
about the errand you needed me to run
and waited to hear about from the cell phone
that was not there in my gray coat pocket.
Once the Hag blurs into her burning bush
all I can do is reach up to the breeze
from the fan above the sheets, turn out right foot first
to grab the floor, and step down to the stoop
and the *New York Times* in the azaleas.
Something that's fit to use from these oracles
relating to the happiness I seek
early among my doings back in this life
comes when I put the pot lids I left to dry,
on the rack beside the sink, in the pan drawer
under the stove without causing a clatter
to wake you up. This triumph of sanity,
if not civility, can set things right
from having gone all wrong until I came.
I sit out on the chair at the wrought-iron table
whose potted begonia centerpiece looks saddened
by a hint of rain against the hazy blue,
and then a few drops on the Arts & Leisure
and little whorls that pock the cream in my tea.
Both cats already crouch wherever they go
and I decamp from my hiding place

to pick up at the sequence from the outset
about the woman with the bright red hair.
The scene broke off with neither of us coming
before we had to grab for our street clothes.
I ponder going back to try again.
She wonders where she put the straw hat she brought
to keep her glossy hairdo from too much sun.
I ask her if she knows where I put the key.
It wasn't in the left-hand camel-hair pocket
packed full of coins and dollar bills and cards
from the people I met all day the day before
who showed me how to get to Baltimore
and its boutique flophouse district near the Métro
I had to go to without key or clue
to find out where it was that you had gone.

Fool

Gorman was living proof that shit does float,
even with slick green streaks in it like a man's
who's drunk too much and said things that he oughtn't.
Some would try to gainsay the constant stench.
Others found colorations of his eyes and affect
that, had they stepped up for a good rich draft
of how he smelled, they'd find that Mickey Gorman
was every bit of shit that he was born as.
Sometimes even he might think he needed
a priest's ear at the grille to apprehend
his too many years of sins venial and bigger.
Only the devil's henchman might sneak a listen
to find out who was next for the sizzling pit,
on account of deeds malodorous enough
their origins had left some traces, like
the sulphur that spoke of Gorman peeking through
the doorway on High Street by the King's Arms,
imparting the King himself with his purple nose
or the King's fool in ragged raiment stained
like the King's own after he'd shat himself
on one of his rouses stumbling like a loony.
It was only Mickey Gorman playing a man,
who gave his best go at a ball of shit
and crawled down to the High to celebrate.
He'd crouch there for a fortnight capably
acting the clown called Shite, who had one word,
not even a line to speak, which he forgot,
then wobbled like a snot-faced runt at the wall.
Had it been mine to do, I would have dropped him
to dine on dandelions by the roots.

But sadly that belonged to a worse rogue,
who grabbed and gutted him in Kirwan's Lane,
and lugged him to the turn by the cheesemonger's,
where somebody had to look for the dead rat.

Art and Life

I know you saw that picture of Courbet's
in the Musée d'Orsay, where everyone
is gathering at the grave of some poor fool,
and the grave is at eye level, in your face.
The coffin's being dragged up with you in it
by an assortment of townspeople in their robes,
sashes, hats, kerchiefs, bonnets, and long looks,
and the day is one great gloom. The coffin's shut
over your face, your secrets, your bare feet.
The hole is open, yawning, freshly dug.
Meanwhile, across the gallery, a mouth
Courbet shaped from a woman's nether parts,
and nothing else, grins at the name he gave them,
L'Origine du Monde. And you laughed out loud.
I never heard you do it, but you did.
A woman with a face no one had seen
and never would again in just that light
had passed along the sidewalk through the rain,
tossing her hair as you stepped out the door
and caught the breeze she shook against your cheek
for the first and last time ever in this life.
I wouldn't try to tell you what you said
under your breath or kept for later on
to tell me, if you had a chance to say it.
There is a sugar maple by your grave,
and a pond across the path that winds around
beside a plot they call Garden of Love.
An old man in a black coat has his back turned.

What Should We Do?

Gratefully, I acknowledged that my doubts had kept me from going all aswim in contentment over such givenness as prevailed everywhere one turned.

MARCEL TOULET

Since everything had gotten so much worse,
I tried to take in at least some one thing
to make out how we came to where we were,
with the result that, on my walk that morning,
which I take solemnly every day, over toward the creek
that rises beyond the highway then disappears
into the forest behind us, to reemerge
two or three blocks away in tiny cataracts
beside a yellow house with a gazebo,
I resourcefully recollected that the French
for *garbage can* sounds like a word for a tiny
blue iris a couple might name their daughter after,
so that when I tried to articulate that moment
in my semiyearly letter to my friend Marcel,
who lives near Montbourbier in the Dordogne,
with its otherworldly river and black cliffside,
I could not imagine how I would convey
with any force in his own vivacious tongue
that we had tumbled into the garbage can of history—
nous sommes tombés dans la poubelle de l'histoire
simply would not do—so I wrote instead
how my wife and I welcomed the news that our plan
to come over to search for leases with options to buy
would coincide with the birth of a new grandchild
who might look back on these as times of triumph,
with or without tumbrels rumbling in order to have it.

An Evening Walk

Inside an ashy flatland the color of dread
I began to savor the way the outside tasted—

a blend of sweet basil and fresh-rubbed thyme,
an erudite soupçon of tarragon in the palate,

a lemony finish that rinsed the senses
in the memory of a walk up a lane in Somerset

between Wrington and Goblin Coombe
beside a yellow pasture with a few cows

downhill from an impetuous purple oak,
a church tower behind it and beyond the tower

blue gone to slate—not many years ago,
scarcely a moment, as events return,

a daw feather fallen into a weave of thorn
among some chestnuts by the roadside.

Saint-Malo

I like to be around people speaking French
to their speckled spaniels at the crêperie
with the *galettes de sarrasin* and a sea-finch
swooping through blurred sun on glossy tiles
under gables and chimney-stacks up near the blue.
I can hear the people and talk back to them
enough to ask them whether the old church
with steeple and gargoyles has been burnt out
since the Second War. It would be nice to know
if I'd come for nothing, looking for Christ's blood
in its golden vial at the cathedral in Fécamp
above Le Havre. I love Le Havre's muscular
exploitation of the eloquence of concrete.
Two hours from surfers' paradise at Omaha Beach,
in Saint-Malo at the Café Gaufrerie Sandwicherie,
Hector crowns my vanilla *glace* in its cornet
with fresh whipped cream and a blue plastic spoon.

The Art of Self-Defense

Another day's stint in the free world
begins here in the donut shop. Standing in line
wondering how many cheese Danish and apple fritters
as well as donuts I should buy, while the creamy girls
in their summer dresses are licking their profiteroles,
I see myself as a boy in the summer of 1953
salting sliced tomatoes with my grandfather
in the white shirt he wore. The kitchen was big and sweet.
The breeze from the electric fan swung by us and away.
The oilcloth on the table was cool and slick.
The leaves of the tree of heaven dappled the sill.
In line in the donut shop is a man in a straw hat
between a woman in pigtails and a boy with large eyes.
Gramps was a boxer in his younger days, semiprofessional.
He watched the Wednesday night fights on our TV.
In his last autumn he taught me to box.
He set up punching bags in his basement.
He taped newspapers to the windows. He named me Spike.
He got me to shadowbox next to the coal bin.
He kept me at it hard till it felt like forever.
When the time came, he arranged a bout
with Mike Donnelly from down the street.
Mike struck the top of my head at once and down I came.
He helped me up from the floor and went home.
I was eleven. I wasn't fast or clever. This was the autumn
after the summer they fried the Rosenbergs.
Gramps walked me down to the corner to get the *Free Press*.
The photograph showed their bodies on the front page.
He tugged my hand and kept me from seeing it.
We mark these solitudes throughout our lives.

This is not simply about things as they are.
This is about donuts, profiteroles, and straw hats.
Things cannot be as they are in this country.

At the Bureau of Divine Music

The whole day I hung around in the sky over Russia
was a Wednesday in October. No one looked up
with any semblance of regard from the heroic Russian people.

I had flown from Paris to visit the faubourgs
of Omsk, Irkutsk, Novosibirsk, but they were filled
with a smother of blue coal fires, shadows of shadows

coughing up tendrils of gray phlegm onto ice floes
that passed for boulevards, back alleys, byways
that ended in country lanes over the Urals

to Ulan Bator and the Mongolian grasslands.
What is the object of going but to bring back free
toothbrushes, peach-bloom porcelains, and colorful boxes

of sandalwood soaps from marble-tiled hotel baths
with the only water pressure in Datong or Yingxian?
Never mind photographs. As my old friend Ray used to say,

tapping his forehead, the pictures you take in here
are the best ones. I don't know how we got there,
but rather than walk back the way we came,

we rambled down the long path from the Temple of Heaven
to a park with sad trees and a moat, and across the moat
a yellow palisade. Nobody else was around.

If unearthly voices fluttered out to us on the swell of wind,
we couldn't hear them. Should the sociopathic cabdriver
drive himself to Heaven after taking us home, his cadaver

would need to be viewed from behind. The star-shaped mole on his left shoulder blade said nothing to anyone. Only two of us, possibly three, remember the tune he often repeated.

The Morning Mail

I gave myself the liberty to stay home
one Monday when I should have gotten dressed
and gone and pulled my end up like a man.
The house got empty after breakfast, which
was not unusual. Weekdays the house stayed empty,
excepting this one, where there was myself,
almost fanatical about the weather,
halfway determined to be under it,
listening for order where there wasn't any
or words for persons not at this address.
After the mailman's truck had come and gone,
the letter from an old Bostonian
pleading for reasons to stay vertical
from those among his fellow countrymen
who took the time to soothe him where it hurt
in the exhausted tissues of the soul,
and speaking with the heart's vernacular,
caused me to lie back down in my bathrobe
to read for evidence of the common life
between us, while the best of us stayed at large.
The living room became a land of dreams,
as of one rainy Monday in Joigny
at the Café République on the main square,
when a woman I knew then kept glancing up
from her café au lait to look around
in every direction except mine,
as if to wonder why we were doing this,
though why we did it neither of us would know,
if ever, till a long time later on,
and in the meantime we would cross the Alps
to Domodossola and Sirmione,

where she would think of how it was in Worcester
and why she had to go there one day soon.
The ship from Rhodes left in the pouring rain.
We slept below on filthy mattresses.
In Athens, two old men in iron chairs
were leaning head to head above their beads
swinging between them, waiting for the train.
The sun came out in Macedonia.
Workmen called one another up and down
after a creaking stop at Leskovac,
cicadas screaming in the station yard.
The beach at Kalamaki near Piraeus
kept coming back to me. There were two women
who led a blind old woman toward the sunup,
and then the three of them, black dresses rolled,
stepped in the water while the old one cried.
Those are her daughters, and they're bathing her
was what we nearly whispered watching them.
Our sleepless night hung heavy on us both.
Voices were coming out of everywhere.
Laden with agony beyond my reach,
the letter dropped behind the davenport.
The time had come to rise up and occur.
I stood beside the window and beheld.
The usual blackbirds on my neighbor's roof
had come to shiver as the rites require.
They were three women, one of them a crone,
leaning together, elbow to elbow,
and one complaining *Sister, she is old—*
we need to take her up and make her fly,
and if she doesn't, maybe she should fall.

And what if they should tumble after her,
leaving their cries to falter in the quiet,
what would they be but black birds tumbling down
to drift above a neighbor's roof again?—
black angels veering in the atmosphere
to look us in our faces where we stand
like empty-handed lovers facing the sea,
wondering why we do this, and how those birds
could fall and keep aloft in the one air.

Do We Never Tire of This?

You had redone the dining room again.
I came downstairs to find my father's urn.
It wasn't under the set of Chinese dogs
on the knickknack in the corner where it was
with the Flemish compote tureen under it
on the Amboise table, and I was miffed a little.
I have more patience to put up with things
than I used to, but only so much this time.
I let my father go for just a while.
There was no hot water, so I took a shower.
It was the morning of the day I would decide
to try to fix the friction at the interface,
which I had regularly gotten mixed up in.
We have a tendency to analyze things too much
I used to say, until I realized
we never actually analyzed things enough.
It was then that I resolved to become the sort
of person upon whom nothing was lost for good.
I stood there in the dining room looking for Dad.
He had made a living as a cattle breeder
until the genetic code of the Galloways
he brought down to Texas ruined everything.
The calves would be born dead and their mothers die
with their eyeballs swollen so they burst.
He blamed it on those goddamned Scottish bulls.
Their pubic hair was on their necks and faces
he always said. I mentioned that to someone once
at a dinner party on the Île Saint Louis.
She folded her serviette like a nun's,
bowed to excuse herself, and stepped outside.

Geometric

Euclid became my savior in tenth grade,
the year the Jesuits wanted me a priest.
They sent me to Manresa in Birmingham
and put me in a room with a radiator
that knocked all night to keep me up for prayer,
nothing for breakfast, not a thing for lunch,
and barley soup and Wonder bread for supper.
It was no wonder then that Euclid cried
out of this darkness of mortification
in a squared circle with a human face
that set me right about four equal lines
drawn from a radius the square root of π,
this being God as Dante painted Him,
and good enough for me to believe in
in place of hellfire and my going there,
because, as I recall, that square was purple,
a color I can see, though color blind,
as I have been since the wet grass was red
after a rain when I was four years old.
That was the spring of 1947.
My grandmother had lathered the lye soap
the way she would when I said damn or shit,
and I ran up the stairs to the closet
I always hid in when she got the suds
and never could find out where I was hiding.
That circled square is purple in my mind
because I can't see Euclid colorless.
This purple borders him upon his throne
of lordly order the geometer
alone encompasses in his mind's eye.

I can't remember whether Euclid ever
attempted squaring the circle, though he must have.
It wasn't something Father Loetze covered.
He was the one before Theology
who told us Euclid looked on Beauty naked,
meaning to shock us, while he tapped the board
in perfect classic Solid Geometry,
his chalky soutane flying with his back turned,
and nothing for it but a reverie
about the breasts of Emil Bogen's daughter
and whether they were perfect cones or spheres.
Her father was a tailor up the street.
He often stood in front on the sidewalk
rolling a piece of chalk between his palms.
He made it crack against his wedding ring.
Behind him the mannequins have nothing on
but open-toed high heels and strings of pearls.

Passage

Some people on it said the ship had breached
the verge of sweet discoveries everyone
aboard would profit from, even the many
who might not get home and those who more than once
had spoken for the freedom to resist
the period style of travel, as I had.
And there was vehemence in what I spoke,
in favor of getting anywhere I pleased
by any means that brought itself to hand,
in this case in the company of a lot
of sodden ne'er-do-wells who paid the booking,
trudged up the gangway, stepped off to the lounge,
and watched the port go under huge cloudbanks
closing the window out of sight of land.
The only one who got me to admit
misgivings as to how my plan would go
was sitting with me over our refreshments.
She seldom even listened in the stateroom
where she would watch the porthole blackening
beyond my voice beside her on my pillow
as she turned over toward oblivion.
What she was thinking when she dubbed the ship
The Ship of Clowns would come clear three days out.
A couple at a table next to us
were staring at their plates scarcely disturbed.
Their waiter asked if he could get them something.
The wife looked to one side, the husband moaned.
Everyone turned aside and started moaning.
All of the tables were one choral moan,
except for ours. Later in bed she said,
"What did you make of that? Could you believe it?"

I took in my own countenance watching me.
For a brisk moment I began to moan.
I had not found a thing to say, I said.
I missed the look of ridicule in her eyes.

Homage

In Andy Warhol's silkscreen rendering
of Leonardo Da Vinci's *The Annunciation*,
the Virgin has her fingers on a book
opened to two front pages the Angel's right
index and middle fingers seem to bless.
The Angel and the Virgin hide their faces.
The painting is a landscape with two hands.
A flagrant sea-green peak sustains the distance,
meaning whatever it is meant to mean.
What book the Virgin has her fingers on
can be submitted to a viewer's choice.
She may not be Ophelia reading her prayers
in readiness for the boyfriend's impudence.
It could be some romance of Da Vinci's day
or Warhol's or the Virgin's for that matter.
The matter here is what God needs from her
by way of a reaction at this time,
seeing her from Eternity by herself
this morning when His messenger gets there
to do exactly what He sent him to,
traverse the thermals the green peak produced
and then to stroll in through the garden gate
to let fall what there was to want of her,
if only something quaintly gestural,
as if she had not wanted what she wanted
and stepped out onto the terrace to have alone,
with no one having to come for any reason—
but to have come that way, and all that way,
to interrupt what she sat down to read,
in its own time, and all unto itself,

that from then on she never could recapture,
no matter how she tried, nor would remember
the thing itself or what she made of it.

Outings

If you don't have it in your own backyard,
go find it somewhere else. Outings are good
to take as randomly as possible.
Go find a table in a restaurant
a town or two away, a corner table
with a view of the whole place. Notice the flower
the owner's mother liked enough to paint
on a canvas twice as big as the TV,
so you can wander on one petal's rim
and slide from there into its white abyss
It's easier to do this close to home,
but never fail to go as far from home
as you can find the means to get. One Sunday
on a clean bench in the Parc du Ranelagh
in the prosperous Seizième Arrondissement
across from the blind Monets in the Marmottan,
I had a double-chocolate ice-cream stick
from the vendor's wagon near the carousel.
I mention that the bench was clean because
most of the benches there had droppings on them,
which was no one's fault. All I had to do
was find a clean spot and a bit of shade
close to the trash bin for the stick and wrapper,
while I woke to the feast of blues and greens.
The rest was autumn and the moms and prams
and boys on bicycles with training wheels.
A girl in a blue dress walked out of the sun
straight up the one long path among the trees
as far as someplace else she had to go.

All You Can Eat

A man is tenderly kissing a child's head.
Across the booth from a gorgeous brown-eyed dolt,
a miraculous young woman is listening.

The fat woman who couldn't stop laughing earlier
at the tall white-bearded man's jokes is remarking now
how scary it was in England during the Blitz.

She makes the sound of a rocket screaming to earth
among shops and pubs and flats and schoolyards,
and everyone at the table is doing it.

Jean-Paul Sartre arrives wearing a leather beret
and jacket, with *Motorpsycho* on the back.
He has in hand a dreadful skinny blond boy

in an electric-blue jumpsuit covered in pink lightning.
It is Les Deux Magots in 1946.
Several tables have people saying grace.

In fact, everyone is praying. The skinny boy hops.
His lightning bolts have batwings and dragon claws.
He hops and hops. His dreadfulness abounds.

The fat woman has died laughing. Her table screams.
The Second World War is over and we all scream.
I seem to be looking around me fearfully.

Ancient Fathers

The town poet and the village idiot met for lunch
on the terrace at the Café de la Gare.
They both were having the soup & salad bar.
"My wife is in Paris," the town poet wept,
"visiting one of her Algerians.
I get no sleep at all, and this makes time
terribly out of joint."—"Time, time—what is it?"
the idiot gasped, erupting around his spoon,
which thoughtfully he slurped before he said:
"And you will never amount to anything,
the reason being that you weep too much,
and, worse, the things you weep about are rot."
The idiot had brought along his dog,
to pick up bits of lettuce from the table.
The dog liked salad. He was an idiot too.
He once said it just felt good to do that.
He spoke a rude *chiènois* only his master knew,
who began to translate: "I think he said
he thinks you are a bigger fool than me.
This dog says words no longer known in Blois,
except among the elders of the Guild,
to which his ancient fathers were house pets.
He is a guard cur—he lives in the woodyard.
The name he called you often was *brutelôt*,
which is a word for carrion dogs don't touch,
and you are the most inedible, he said.
You won't stop weeping, either."—"I would stop,"
the poet said, "if your dog—what's his name?"—
"Gaston," the idiot enthused, "his name's *Gaston*."—
"If Gaston would drag up someone's left leg,

chewed off above the thigh," the poet said,
"I'd stop." He shook a tear toward Gaston,
who was a festive little Papillon,
and dropped both fists onto the ground and barked.

Celebrant

Here is a realm of swollen chestnut trees
emptying their hands on the Great Lawn,
where figures enter toward a unison
of need, immaculate as chalices
sipped, wrung dry, shut up, the key in the sleeve,
the broken priest gone home to dine alone.
The tea things on the trays know why these people
steal in from white skies cursorily breaking gray
above the torpor they behold and bear.
Nothing of what they found by the lakeside
or in the little pinewood trembling there
in specks of shine and shadow offers them
much they can name or note before they rise.
Someone all wan immediacy is peering
through the beveled pane above the window seat
on the garden side of the drawing room
at the monkey puzzle by the folly
the patriarch had built to show the locals
what a great treat Attic architecture
could be to look at in the wintertime—
and the first snowflake actually falls.
The face in the glass is the patriarch's,
who used to visit the boathouse through a tunnel
unknown to the servants or her ladyship.
A man with a pipe and a woman lost
in a chapter about the son-and-heir's return
three hundred pages after he was born,
and never heard from until now, look up.
She asks to be excused inaudibly,
leaving the man with the pipe to watch the person
by the window, who has seen thousands of flakes

obscuring the temple of Artemis
so that his own face becomes all there is.
The two of them linger in communion
of a depth they never can begin to deepen.

Hermitage

I had not fit my mind around the things
she needed me to do or answer for,
nor had I come to notice where she went,
which meant I had not thought to look for her.
No words were spoken that were any good,
nor any said to make good what was not.
My spite for almost everyone in town,
including her and me, had taken on
a numbness like an anchorite's in a cave.
I often saw myself as such—on Gozo,
which seemed the kind of perfect fourth-rate place
to go and live, above a stretch of coast,
alone, or with a woman in a smock,
who'd feed me every other day or so
a simple meal of octopus and chips
washed down with local currant wine well chilled
from a sweaty beaker of aluminum.
She'd chop the tentacles in lengths like sausage,
set them on a bright blue plate with peppers
and cucumbers beside the cup of wine.
She'd watch me eat without a word and wait
until I sat there staring at the sea
in one of my redoubtable abstractions
while she ducked down the path back to the village.
The way these sons of bitches chop you up
and hand you little bits of you to eat
had left me silence as my only portion,
dredged in a complex seasoning of rage.
I had no reason to apologize
for what I did or was about to do.
My feeling state was mine and theirs was theirs.

As for herself, all I could do was go.
It was the pure clear light of June that watched it,
the way it can in the Dodecanese
between the rainy season and the hordes
that loose themselves from where it is they were
to go about their business on the beaches
in company with everybody else
likewise inclined, for however long they please,
while someone like myself would just as soon
go one way or the other on my own,
obliged to no one and in my own way,
and glad to be there or be rid of it
when riddance would be good and I could get it.
Kalymnos came to mind among the places
to simply disappear without a word,
as long as there was one more mountain path
to follow, up among the figs and crickets,
with blue above it bluer than any blue.
The short way out stood ready in the doorway.
The long one found a district of one-way streets
and detours into fields of disused airstrips
from which the crows shocked themselves into flight
to catch a load of leaves to perch among
and shout recriminations, reprehensions,
or cries for war and bits enough to dine on.

The Consecration of the House

I took a soak November 22nd.
John Kennedy was dead forty-five years.
I would be sixty-five in the same month's time
it took me to turn twenty-one that year
and go out with my father for a drink
at Tommy Burke's on Vernor in Detroit.
There I was in the tub we have upstairs
and thinking on the soul in good hot water,
the way some lines of Yeats advised me to,
and I felt certain it was about time,
a bit too late, or both, or none of these.

That morning I read "The Gift of Harun Al-Rashid."
Kusta ben Luka—doctor, philosopher—
unburdens to a Christian friend of his,
and tells him how the gift the Caliph brought him
could sleeptalk on a range of sacred matters
his age had driven him to care about,
regardless of what had seemed impossible,
along with things the girl could do awake
that made him wonder what the Caliph meant.
Before half of this monologue elapses,
Kusta reveals how certain people's souls
appear to radiate from within their bodies.
I longed to learn exactly how that happens,
which ministered to an impulse to search out
Parmenides' or Yeats's allegory
left on the bookshelf where the Caliph kept
genial visions to be sought for comfort.
Somebody here knew something worth the knowing.

And here it was a Saturday in November,
with the first fire down in the grate, my wife
working her crossword puzzle, me in the tub,
the sun sparkling the window in the bathroom,
the weather apt to warm up later on.
I kicked the suds around until they died.
The quiet dropped again. And then I knew
why water is the generated soul,
and why from downstairs Ann would ask to find
the word *to be* in French, which I spelled out,
and added, "It's also the word for *being*,
as in *L'Être et le Néant* by Jean-Paul Sartre,"
as if she welcomed too much information,
which in that case I was quite sure she hadn't.
"And don't forget the circumflex on the *E*."
"How did I know you'd tell me that?" she said.
I thought she said it. I could not be sure,
for all the house between us and the way
the waters round had calmed me body and soul,
to keep on going onward, at a loss.

It wasn't about that day or the day's date.
Nothing about it was what we thought it was.
To keep on being or to be or not
to be were not the matter. They were all
beside the point. Once we had got the point,
the point itself would be beside the point.
When Kennedy took a sharp left onto Elm,
seconds before his brains burst from his head,
time went off where it came from, leaving him

the moment that his soul had left to shine
through him and out of him. The overpass
would darken him soon enough out of sight,
into more quiet than he knew already.

Old Money

I bought a Roman silver denarius
at Hudson's Department Store in Detroit,
with a week's collection from my paper route
when I was twelve. Marcus Aurelius
still looks surprisingly like one of us,
approaching sixty, and a little tired
from things that kept him always on his guard.
He seems to be there just the way he was
after the middle of the Second Century,
and in the seventeenth year of his reign:
one of the nicest tyrants in history
having to glance away from everyone,
who never got to know him personally,
passing from palm to palm on a gray coin.

Midwinter Day

Every time I ask this the answer comes
and says I missed it too long a time ago
to do one thing to change it at that time
and time was what it needed. It is time
we haven't got that it needs now, and when
we had it, it was not the kind of time
we thought we wanted, so we did not know,
or care to, that this kind of time was all
the time we had or even would have had.
Time would have told us this if time could tell.
Time doesn't tell as much as time is told.
Time only does what time is going to do.
Time couldn't tell. Time never does. Time won't.
Time can't begin to tell until time can't.

Hearth

I tried to read the smoke from the chimney
to see if she had waked and put more sods on.
The puff of white at first said one thing, then
a long spell of none at all said otherwise.
It could have been the top sod I had set
that fell into the embers and made smoke.
What made me turn around and want to look
was what she might be thinking had I kept
on walking down the road past cottages
that held the ground in townlands on beyond
the rise there with its spectacle of sea,
and then what I would do and where to go
was anyone's idea, even mine or hers,
the way she watched and pondered at the window.

A Cry

A cry came from someplace beyond the yard.
Though the intended good of what to do
was less than obvious straight off, I listened.
For a moment afterward the cry and I
kept our own kindred mornings in July.
Its lack of agony was unabashed.
Its sound kept up awhile, exact and small.
Whose trees it rose amongst I could not tell.
Soon I repaired upstairs to disappear,
then went back down, prepared to find it gone.
In fact, I never heard from it again.

Except for my three-legged cat, who slept
on the chaise lounge, the dog and her own cat
simply went off and shat, one in the bamboo,
the other on the new grass near some holes
the rain made merely to cause me some bother.
Nothing took place that seemed the least the matter.
My current status with the imbeciles
who counted foremost this millennium
composed a state of near complete aplomb.
Illusions came and went this way and that,
till a great many things had run together.

It made me keep the sadness of January
pacing about my heart's chilliest room,
with a door that opened the wrong way out
onto the abysmal sweep of a stairwell.
The likelihood of becoming an old soul
like me would frame itself as time pressed on,
if I could manage to produce insouciance

amidst my droll display of nonchalance
and strength to strive by in the undertow
effort will soon enact against a person,
regardless of the style of one's ado.

Later I looked out over the whole town
from a good spot to watch the sun go down
behind a dingy glimpse of countryside.
The huge flag at the Autopark was bigger
than the drive-in movie's screen on up the road.
I surely love to just enjoy the view.
This time I stood and walked around in it.
I did this better than I thought I would.
I came to flow throughout the space I trod
and looked from at the kingdom of July.
Anyone listening could have heard a cry.

The Breaking of the Day

1

Whole neighborhoods of people happier
than I am wake up stepping toward their doors
and opening, then staring at the air
that slips in, bearing tidings unawares.
Their cats and dogs will sit around and think.
They never tell the people anything.
They could just sit and look around and blink.
There should be more than that: birds on the wing,
light seeping through the trees, squirrels seeking nuts,
three-toed box turtles courting. Speaking of cats,
my cat can think and blink as well as any.
He knows he has a life as good as money.
And speaking of Monet, he has it all.
His *Bridge at Giverny* is wonderful.

2

A good part of the day that broke just then
has disappeared already. We are still here,
my cat and I. He's on the other chair
taking a nap. I will, this afternoon.
When I wake up at 6 a.m., I'm up.
There is no point in lying there in bed
as if I need to practice being dead.
I know when I have had enough of sleep.
But later on this afternoon I will—
either upstairs, where it is dark and cool,
or out here in the yard—I'll shut it off.
The hour or two I missed will be enough.
Bright green against deep blue makes me relax.
I love the way the hammock rocks and creaks.

3

It is not easy being the grandson
of the great patriarch. He is in the sky,
for one thing; I am not. I try and try,
but I am still below, very far down
upon the earth. The angel said as much
when he bestowed that little agony,
and even though he kicks you in the crotch,
you will not let him go without a cry
of blessing on you and your nether spawn.
It tells the generations. It brings the pain
that follows us around. It is my thigh
each time I try to move it off the couch.
Run where I might, I never will outrun
the dread that rises deep inside that bone.

A Bar of Chinese Soap

I wanted to speak of something you could use,
when you got to be my age. This is not far
from where you are, as you might think it is.
With adequate cerebral attributes
such as you possess, along with richnesses
of wherewithal, the prospect clarifies,
so someone just a bit long in the tooth
could come to notice how many old fools
as well as old wise men there are around.
Both of them miss the truth. The truth is hard.
One does grow used to looking on them both
with like disdain. This can be taught and learned.
Whatever goes there, bee and flower will join
the ministries of sense from their two forms.

Awake

I lay down in my bed and went to sleep
but only after worrying that the pain
that came up in my chest, seemingly deep
inside it where my heart was, was a plain
signal that I might not survive the night
and could be lying cold beside my wife
when she got up, as she does, with the light,
to start another day in her own life,
while mine was over, unbeknown to us,
including me. As I was worrying,
I went to sleep and woke up in four hours
to use the bathroom. Birds had begun to sing.
Two dogs were barking. Nothing perilous
had come to find us. What was ours was ours.

Purple

I may need to recall the given year
this happened, if it's different than I thought.
All I need do is sit back on the chair
I have beside the old table I bought,
and look up at the ceiling with my hands
hanging down loosely backward, as at ease
as I can be in the sharp part of my brains
where I keep most of my liveliest ideas,
sometimes before I even put them down,
and often without ever doing that,
so I take one of them and look at it—
in this case it's the one about my death
and whether there had been a sliver of sun
on the purple wall. And I take a breath.

Acknowledgments

Thanks are due the publishers of the following journals for permission to reprint:

The Aroostook Review: "A Bar of Chinese Soap" and "Awake"

Crowd: "Hermitage" and "The Consecration of the House"

First Things: "Outings"

The Little Balkans Review: "Tahiti"

Margie: "Geometric," "Ancient Fathers," and "All You Can Eat"

Measure: "Save Yourself," "Campanile," and "Fool"

Mêlée: "The Art of Self-Defense"

Poetry: "At the Bureau of Divine Music"

Poetry Ireland Review: "Purple"

The Quarterly: "The Morning Mail"

Shenandoah: "The Dove"

The Southern Review: "Eclogue"

Third Coast: "The Scent of Rose Water"

Typo: "The Empress"

Unsplendid: "The Way You Do" and "Celebrant"

Willow Springs: "A Sudden Shower"

Wolf Review: "The Breaking of the Day"

"The Message" originally appeared in *The Routledge Anthology of Cross-Gendered Verse,* ed. Alan Michael Parker and Mark Willhardt (London: Routledge, 1996); "Africa" in *Visiting Frost: Poems Inspired by the Life and Work of Robert Frost,* ed. Thom Tammaro and Sheila Coghill (Iowa City: University of Iowa Press, 2005); "Art and Life" in *For, From, About James T. Whitehead,* ed. Michael Burns (Springfield, MO: Moon City Press, 2009); and "Old Money" in *IOU: New Writing on Money,* ed. Ron Slate (Concord, MA: Concord Free Press, 2010).